GENERAL MOTORS

GENERAL MOTORS

Ryan Eckes

General Motors © 2018, Ryan Eckes. All rights reserved. No part of this book may be used or reproduced without consent from the author or publisher except in the case of brief quotations appropriated for use in articles and reviews.

Published by Split Lip Press
333 Sinkler Road
Wyncote, PA 19095
www.splitlippress.com

ISBN: 978-1984332998

Cover Concept by Brandon Eckes
Cover Photo by John Burke
Cover Design by Jayme Cawthern

table of contents

I   chase scenes   -   3

II   spurs   -   25

III   strikes   -   46

I   chase scenes

we're in a classroom, which is a store. the professor tells us the true
writer must destroy his own ego. do not tell stories, he says, unless
they are someone else's. do not say i. i look at the clock and the clock's
the wind. it says one tongue per king, and that pulls on me like a sad
movie. i just watched five easy pieces, what a bummer. what a bummer
he left her and life up in the air like a dead piano. i'm sick of the road
as the end as if no gas station rots forever round the bend. one tongue
per king, the poem becomes its own thing. not america, not this professor
pulling maps down over the board, pretending to stand outside. he's
the enemy, which is at least tens of thousands of people. i'm not looking
for the enemy. we look at each other and pass notes. call on me, call
on me. let's see what happens.

we're in mcglinchey's dancing to the juke box, iggy pop. *no dancing,* says bartender, but we keep dancing, the waitress comes over, *for real stop dancing or you gotta leave.* it's the law somehow, but we're drunk and we want you, come dance w/ us, please—please be the girl we used to love way way back, she won't crack the slightest smile. i don't know who i'm even talking to. is this a poem? a poetry reading? she drags my dead horse across the bar and says *look, who wants this joke. you think it's my job to listen to you, it's not—it's to serve you hot dogs while you drink yourself back to the womb—which is what—you don't know, and that's your job—to find out. i am not the passenger. i do not ride and ride and ride.*

we're in the steamfitters hall peeling walmart stickers off hundreds of copies of the mark of athena. athena will be free, and kids will love her, and kids will leave her for the sea of monsters, and the sea of monsters 2. *you can't get away from blue*, a little girl tells me. then here we are—blue—blue rolls the street thru as each april will. to mess you up a little. a little april pointed at the wrong people. over production. over the rainbow, the luxury of committing to nothing. blue peels off. liberty motel, liberty gas. liberty thru and thru.

what's wiseblood? all the cleverness, all the being-outside-of. wawa goose flies thru it and the vulture brains fall away. i am a person of septa, laugh at me. everybody knows captain moneybags was hired to dj the conversation, that's fine: half-assed foreplay and the great depression. knife on the roof, been there seven years. blood to rust. so what should the maximum wage be? cockroach the size of an alligator just slid under my radiator.

we're in a chik-fil-a spiking the sweet tea w/ birth control. the deep state of cumming hard spreads an all caps hush of southern hospitality. finally i get it. we can barely contain ourselves. hell dies, who wants coffee? all day the drip in my step elects the ground i walk on—a joke you can bite like a peach. see the coins we trust in—those are gods passed out on the bathroom floor.

we're in applebee's, and you have a gun. okay. high art lives, the stomach is greased. am i talking too matter-of-factly about suicide? there's a reason wal-marts and pet-smarts keep popping up all over: it's hero time, still. your daughter's getting sleepy, the bus boy wants to take her home. watch out—he don't pay taxes, never will. look at him, shredding our right to work. what if we didn't have a right to work. sure i'll read your broke-ass poem for the fourth time. let's let this place be paradise before the next round of fires. take off all your clothes, and put your hands on my head.

we're in a greyhound station in baltimore w/ an hour to kill, staring at the tv. cnn is in love w/ the bombing of the boston marathon, and cnn is in love w/ 165,000 new jobs, 165,000 new jobs, 165,000 new jobs. they zoom in to their analyst who's been staring at the mayor's face. i can see the mayor's tears, he says, the mayor means it. he'll make a wonderful ronald reagan some day, just as the last four presidents, just as the president today who picks up your phone—anybody there? anybody says "my dumb life" but in the station and on the bus nothing rings and nobody means a thing, so we're a tribe. it's communism, calm as a yawn til the next city, where we'll be sucked out and dispersed by vacuums of identity. finally we board. the man next to me asks if i can watch his bag. sure i can.

we're in toon town. gag orders pause a judge up the creek like
a FREE sign taped to garbage. your life is whose? the trees sneeze
and cough, we're all dirty water, minor poets. it's a certain kind
of person expects to be cleaned up after—everybody, anybody
lurching for the jackpot. i hit it, jessica rabbits hop all over me,
make one great jessica rabbit. in her mouth all weeks leak out
thighs for sleep, no wait. rent paid then monday heaves, shucks
hi and this malaise you'll forget—now, which could be anything—
amargi, sumerian word for freedom, *return to mother*, literally. you
die, love, whatever, still my friends are buildings. they fight off
despair all the time, all the time. in their bricks heat of sadness
of capitalism, god! fuck it—*to the beaches, the look of beaches in our
faces, okay—zero killed—oceans, oceans, oceans—down to earth, earth,
earth—*

why does your milkman whistle in the morning? because church is a puddle we piss in together—no debts. no drinkus interruptus. LA's gone under, thank god, before new orleans. a toast to the ice on our tail—chase it til hard work melts the carousel of progress and we'll swap spits like grandparents atop new year, stop being the thing we were thought into. 11:59 pops into 12:00, looks fake but isn't. as if you were ever a citizen of anything. be proud of your friends and the luck between you—call it a country, even, til you gag on it—because you are a fool, and fools go on.

we're sitting in sallie mae's driveway in delaware, arms locked singing songs to cops in stupid hats. they won't let us in the shareholders' meeting because we're not rich and we don't believe in fucking people over. our heads are getting burned up in the sun but we keep singing to the cops and to ourselves. then all at once the hundred of us blow our little red whistles that say SLAP, deafening everything—excruciating, it's excruciating, the cops are cursing at us, *oh shit! i would give you a trillion dollars to make it stop. i would give you five million lamborghinis, 15,000 private jets, 140 private islands and every team in baseball one trillion times. i would give you one trillion decades of war in a country you'll never have to see. sallie mae, i would feed you the corpse of your mother, inch by fucking inch.*

we're in jingo pipeline heaven, and you are a cloud, so get in the car. there is no "becoming." the poets, handcuffed, police each other's authenticity. their world shrinks to a nugget. bukowski's tombstone: don't try. nickels and dimes, the wheels on the bus, which is us. when you say "who you are," the sources hurt, the irony fails. if a word's a flag, just stick it in the ground, walk out the cemetery. don't stick it on your car. your car will be towed. it will be towed by a christian single. what is a christian single?

we're on record, skipping around in the washington post amazon buys. the store greeter hawks a poetics. what is love? the answer: heavy possibility, the sag of the feeling of a time you miss, the balls full of cum—the *the-the-the*, that's all. in other words, monopoly. the year we did not see each other's faces. in other words, wrong question. that shit is adjunct, hole of the essential. like a septa we sunk our life into. that tease of the page-to-page life. listen, where we left off i was saying don't play basketball when i'm talking about heraclitus. but you play basketball. and i talk about heraclitus. we dribble in the same river twice. the river is broke and the blackbird is flying. the adjunct, my friend, is blowing in the wind.

we're up 18-0, too bad it doesn't count. i'm there in spirit, says someone clinging to nothing, muted field mown brown to the dead who swim underground. every passing stranger hooks to every passing stranger—anger, the sea. history of some "pure present" we can wave to in the window. both arms are acceptable. the history of how to swim begins with drowning. our mannequin comes up for breath, it's monday. we chase fragments. we will never kill all of these fascists. we are a they, looted, so go ahead and cheers with your water. that's the heart holding out. *that's some pete rosey shit*, you say. you whisper, without a contract, *i have no bosses in this room.* the room is hunger. we swallow.

we're surviving, so there's a show. some lines i grow jealous of. bills flow thru my body, wet day dreams. you can have that line. make it stroll out the mouth of a fish. see something, say something. i wasn't expecting to be moved by the zombies, but i was. the vast pastures of irrelevance. the pervasive motorization of petty individualisms. their detours of pleasure scribbled in hurry—those streets await our faith. we can have them. like the birds. birds are pervs. pervasive motorization, one tweets. one squawks. one fucks.

we're doing unpaid work in the courtroom while temple university's lawyer attacks us for being poor. his tongue is a wet dollar. *you have no power,* he says, *it says so right here in this poem you didn't write. therefore, you should have no power— you can just go home.* but we just sit there and we can't be fired for just sitting there, for being a poet, for being a union. for being an army of lovers. the lawyer's tongue is then a wet piece of toilet paper. part of it tears off and falls to the floor. pick it up, says the judge. the lawyer picks up his tongue and hands it to the provost, who puts it in his own mouth and begins to chew. wet shit runs down his chin, dribbles onto his tie. the judge orders a five-minute break. outside the provost tries to shake my hand, so i hand him a fish, which he begins smacking on the pavement, smacking the fish on the pavement over and over and he begins to choke, choking on the poem we didn't write. and we stand there and watch the provost choke and choke and then, finally, die. then, on his forehead, we write a big fucking F.

we're a hammer in the radiator, naming every instant of collective joy—in person, in person, to make the platform each nothing and pulsing, a sea of exes on a ship of toothpicks so the music's a question to match all the preaching. passenger pigeon to joe jerk-off: can we just be people. then a quick row of faces—nope, nope, nope, nope it's just fall, a hole in the iris like a ten-cent cloud of witness, and what evidence. transpass, leaf under shoe, wawa gift card, a "moderate" who tells us to "keep working on that message." *let's dump out his coffee! dump that motherfucker already—yes him to death, yes him to death!*

we're in old city unsnapping the horses' shitbags. freedom is free, the street buckles like empties. the tourists, white, turn red as gum— it behooves them. corona pony for you, corona pony for me—cheers to brick wall, full dues paid against which i smash myself into our empties—openness, then, salt on the lips. whims of higher ups just pissed into cups, beer pong for the board of trustees who buck like starved asses in a jar of nothing. in a jar of fake history. it rolls down the street, halts at a fence of paul revere droppings. *shhh, shhh!* let the sewer speak.

i don't know anything about horses. pet the bus w/ your breath. window, go, it's me. runs like new. what does love want from me. before standard time a horse beat a train called tom thumb in a race, 1830. train broke down under moon, horse had no name— that's time. old pain, moon, round and round. the horse's eyes roll back, run away. my mother's last name is west, it's empty. she escaped it, laboring for everyone after her father lost his job at quaker rubber, drank himself to nothing. we could reinvent the whole disaster. my car is parked outside. i was born on february 42nd. i sat way in the back of the horse's mouth for twelve years w/ my heart on fire. the future means no. the rest is history i will rip apart w/ you.

we're driving down washington ave, listening to "wonderful tonight." do i feel all right? i feel the dumpy heat, red light every fifty feet. sad horns from the corners dismember the clapton, cluck-u-chicken. cluck-u-seven eleven. cluck-u-a-plus mini mart. i remember, right around here, losing my breath once from heartbreak, out of nowhere, just walking along here, at night. frozen music. architecture is frozen music. people were drinking in the scoreboard, which is closed. we closed it, remember, to drink inside and watch people kiss and turn off the lights and be washington ave.

good luck in all your future endeavors, types the middle manager chewing on a slim jim. back at home we're rinsing off the isms. it's the wknd, and the middle class are out volunteering for the one percent. we grow free w/out them, though they keep calling. feel them push monday into sunday, friday into saturday. one percent of one smidgen of a dead cockroach's heart casts its vote, finally, for the middle class. can freedom be a pigeon? if it kicks you the right way. if it spits on your shoe and laughs in your face. if in your neighbor's face you look long enough to lose your mask, and you feel it fly away, feel it shit on a boss—any boss—then yes.

we're playing chess on the unfinished concourse to nowhere. you take off your gas mask and look at me. a train slides under us, the heart flutters, the homeless who sleep in waves around us. are we homeless, you say, the city unridden in your face, the lines unbuilt. you want to organize the ocean. unwrap the fish, i say. you unwrap the fish, and the fish squints. we begin where we are. the king is dead, and the queen is dead, and the night is fat with pawns.

II spurs

In 1912, Philadelphia's transit commissioner, A. Merritt Taylor, proposed a comprehensive subway plan to serve the transit needs of the entire city of Philadelphia. Only two of the proposed subway lines were ever completed: the Market-Frankford line (1922) and the Broad Street line (1938; extended slightly in 1956 & 1973). Plans for other lines were revised/revived over the years but ultimately abandoned.

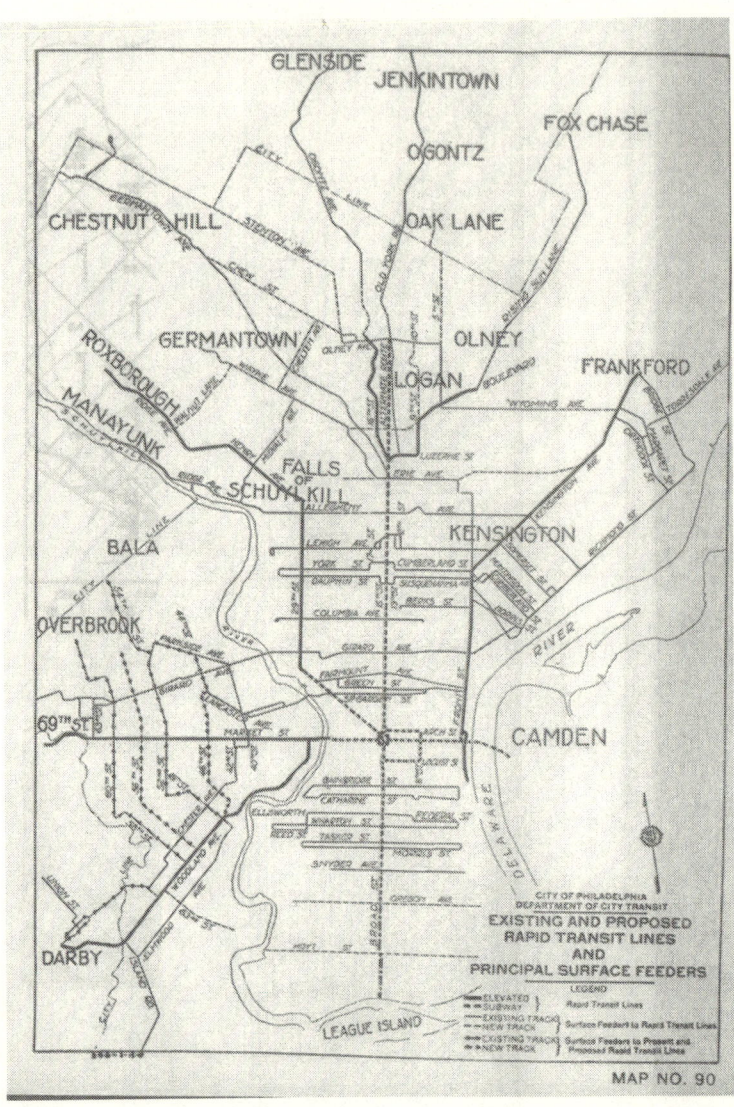

Passyunk spur

There was a plan for a Passyunk spur off the Broad Street line in South Philly. It would run southwest under Passyunk Ave, all the way out, maybe, to Tinicum, the wildlife preserve at the edge of the city, home to freshwater tidal marsh, migratory birds, ducks, deer, fish, foxes and other small animals.

Before the wildlife was "preserved," of course, all of South Philly was wild. *Weccacoe*, it was called by the Lenape. That's supposed to mean "peaceful place."

But this English word, "peace," derives from the Latin *pax*, which means binding together (fastening) by treaty or agreement, as in *pact*. So "peace," rooted in some idea of boundary and nation, unties my faith in the translation.

The past remains wild.

I hear the word "wild" in Stevie Nicks' voice.

Don't blame it on me
Blame it on my wild heart
she sings to me

Whose heart is not a wild heart, I wonder. And if you are not your heart, then what are you?

And who, afraid of violence, does not become violent? I try to raise my hand. It trembles from the violence my body's absorbed, the violence in my blood, the violence in my memory.

Everybody's got a hungry heart
Bruce Springsteen sings
to everybody
in the stadium
at the end of
the line
it means nothing

An artist I know who made my own heart grow wilder told me once in a bar that her favorite love song is "Tougher than the Rest" by Bruce Springsteen, from his album *Tunnel of Love*.

Soon after, I stumbled on a *Tunnel of Love* cassette tape in a used record store. I played it in my car every day, to and from work, for several months, until it hurt too much. I replaced it with The Supremes' *Right On* and played it every day, to and from work, until it hurt too much.

This isn't about what could have been, but the past bores a hole in my heart, and I write into it, as if entering a tunnel.

The juke box plays, and people try to say what it means in the background.

I don't know all that I know. I know lovers sometimes need restraining orders. I know the difference between *inhibit* and *inhabit* is very slim. Both derive from the Latin *habēre*—to hold, possess, have, handle.
There is no place like home.

When I hear *Weccacoe* I think first of Weccacoe Avenue, home to the Philadelphia Parking Authority at the bottom of the city, where they tow your car. It's hard to get to if you don't have a ride. It's hard to get your car back. Why should we give it back to you, you piece of shit. You fucking animal.

OCF Realty recently advertised a new condo called "Weccacoe Flats." Like the parking authority, OCF is expert at fucking over the poor. They're responsible for much of South Philly's gentrification, especially in the black neighborhood Point Breeze.

There's a corner store called Wicacco on 4th St. in Queen Village. I've occasionally stopped there for a bottle of water on my way to South St.

Around the corner from the corner store is Weccacoe Playground. Under the playground is the Bethel Burying Ground, where 5,000 African Americans were laid to rest during the first half of the nineteenth century by the Mother Bethel African Methodist Episcopal Church. The church remains as the oldest Black-owned church in the country, though the neighborhood was gentrified long ago.

The word "cemetery" derives from the Indo-European root *kei-*, which means *bed, couch* and also *beloved, dear*. The words *city, civic, civil, cite, incite, excite* and *resuscitate* derive from this same root.

Every word is a spur, an outgrowth, a departure. Language, like the city, is wild, even while it inhibits our freedom, our ability to make peace.
I think *Weccacoe* now means this: to make poor, or to systematically fuck the poor.

There is no peace.

Passyunk Avenue was once a footpath, I learned from Kevin Varrone's book *Passyunk Lost*. I got lost in it. In my own neighborhood. Which I do not possess. Which no one does but the dead.

I know I can't leave. I want to go inside this city I was born into, but I want somewhere other than cemetery.

A spur is the track of an animal. I try to follow.

Right now we're heading into winter. I would like to speed thru it. I would like to be able to get out of bed in the morning and just do my job.

I want you. I want you. I want you, peaceful place.

Germantown spur

There was a plan for a Germantown spur off the Broad Street line that would take off from Erie Station in North Philly and run northwest under Germantown Ave. Germantown was once German Township, two words, a distant suburb where textile mills lined Wissahickon Creek. In the 19th century it was pulled into Philly by the railroad as the city pushed outward as if trying to escape itself.

Germantown is many histories of escape, of refuge and flight. There was a station on the Underground Railroad in the 1850s, right on Germantown Ave, known as the Johnson House. It still stands, now a museum.

Museum means "shrine of the muses," an attempt at making a house of mind, a station for thinking. So it can't work the way you want it to. Muses move, pass through. A station wants you to stay, to stand like a steed in a stable.

"A museum is a curious graveyard of *thinking*," wrote Amiri Baraka in his essay "Hunting is not those heads on the wall."

In the 1790s, George Washington whose head is on the quarter and one-dollar bill escaped Philly's yellow fever epidemic by hiding in Germantown, along with other rich people, 6 miles away from the city. Horses and boats took them there. Horses were status symbols.

Imagine the man on the one-dollar bill petting his favorite horse. *This one's my favorite*, he says. Imagine him, with that one-dollar expression, naming his horse. *This is Mary Ball*, he says, *I love her*. Imagine the man on the one-dollar bill talking to his horse. *It's all right, baby, we're almost there*.

Money turns you into a cartoon, a rubber band that can be shot across the room, bounced into other forms. Time does this too. So does speed and the desire for speed—that you must *be* traffic to escape traffic. No one thinks of themselves as traffic, even while they're *in* traffic.

As traffic, you're part of your vehicle and part of everyone else's. As you speed up, you embody the freedom you desire, escape itself, the pleasure of animation, wind blowing in your face, and you become more elastic, more fluid, like Tom or Jerry, like the Road Runner, like Wile E. Coyote, and you begin to feel more and more invincible. You fly on I-95 as pure spirit until traffic slows, and then slows, and then comes to a standstill, and you want to pull your hair out, because you're a cartoon just like everyone else, in your private car, melting into the public roads, which will never be yours.

Fuck you and the horse you rode in on.

Fuck me and the Ford Focus I broke down in.

We gotta get out of this place / If it's the last thing we ever do / We gotta get out of this place / Girl, there's a better life for me and you

That's the Animals, 1965. Bruce Springsteen, "The Boss," has said, "That's every song I've ever written. That's all of them. I'm not kidding, either. That's 'Born to Run', 'Born in the USA'."

It's a song born of working-class frustration. It's not a song about overthrowing capitalism but of escaping it. It's a song you turn up in traffic, where solidarity is impossible. You are stuck in the hellish city. Stuck in your job. Stuck in your body, slaving away just like your mother and father, just like your neighbor. Nothing but traffic. Animals in need of animation.

The words "animal" and "animation" share the word "anima," which means "soul." The Indo-European root, *anə*, means "to breathe."

In the film noir *Who Framed Roger Rabbit* (1988), humans and cartoons co-exist. It's the 1940s, and in contrast to the humans, cartoons are playful, imaginative beings—artists—who live more or less peacefully with one another in a completely animated part of Los Angeles called Toontown. They are also immortal unless erased by a special "dip." All of Toontown is under threat of erasure because of a plot to build a freeway through it. To make it happen, Judge Doom has purchased LA's public streetcar system in order to destroy it.

Judge Doom's dream is our reality: "I see a place where people get on and off the freeway. On and off. All day, all night. Soon where Toontown once stood will be a string of gas stations, inexpensive motels, restaurants that serve rapidly-prepared food, tire salons, automobile dealerships, and wonderful, wonderful billboards reaching as far as the eye can see. My God, it'll be beautiful."

Fortunately, the good guys win. The human protagonist, detective Eddie Valiant, saves the animated protagonist, Roger Rabbit, and in doing so he helps save Toontown. He also regains his lost sense of humor and breaks his own depression. He gives Roger a big funny kiss and all the toons cheer as they've won collective ownership of Toontown. In the end, Valiant finds his *anima*. The movie, ultimately, is about fending off spiritual death. Implicit is a critique of Jim Crow-era racism—toons, who are drawings of animals, including people, are discriminated against, seen as *less than human*, and are segregated from humans, who believe they themselves are *not-animals*.

In real life, Judge Doom was General Motors, which along with Standard Oil, Firestone Tires, Mack, and Philips Petroleum, conspired to dismantle streetcar systems across the USA in the 1930s and 40s. They succeeded by using a front company called National City Lines. I learned this on 11th St. one day waiting for the 23 bus, which takes you to Germantown. The bus was late and the man next to me, who was complaining about SEPTA, started musing about the long-gone wonderful days of streetcars, how they ran up every street before we had buses. He told me to look up National City Lines. I did.

A hundred years ago, Philly had 550 miles of track and a fleet of 2,000 trolleys. Then came the rise of the car, which is an eraser. Then came the Great Depression. Then National City Lines: most trolley routes were converted to buses. And subway development slowed. Then came World War II and highways and suburbs, blockbusting and white flight.

In real life, Eddie Valiant and Roger Rabbit were people who drove cars, listening to Bruce Springsteen songs before Bruce Springsteen was born.

There were people in Germantown like Samuel West, my great-grandfather who made a living at the BUDD factory, which manufactured train and car bodies. His father, Thomas West, had drunk himself to death after the Great Depression sunk his textile mill and lightning killed his eldest son on the roof of their house. The rest of the family fought over the scraps and Samuel wanted nothing to do with it. He eloped with a poor girl from Scranton, moved to another neighborhood. He never talked to his siblings again.

For Samuel, love was an escape. His granddaughter, Dorothy, is my mother. She says Samuel loved his new family but was close-minded and racist. He told her once, whichever political party is in power, join that party—that way, you know someone's got your back when things get bad. To him, all politicians were crooks. Their ideas didn't matter. What mattered was self-preservation.

Having escaped, Samuel found himself preserved, happy with where he was, sitting on his small piece of land in North Philly, believing perhaps that he was his own boss, pretending perhaps not to be erasing anything. But the world began to swirl around him again, and he started to feel that he couldn't move, that he was stuck as if he were in a museum and people were looking in but could not see him. And he began to panic.

Center City loop

-Looks like we just missed one.

-Yep. Miss it every night.

Northeast spur

There was a plan for a Northeast spur off the Broad Street line that would take off from Erie Avenue and run under Roosevelt Boulevard to the end of the city. In 1912, when a citywide subway system was originally proposed, Bustleton, where I grew up, was still farmland and the Boulevard was still being built. The Boulevard would become part of the Lincoln Highway, also conceived of in 1912, a transcontinental highway running from Times Square in NYC to Lincoln Park in San Francisco, warping time and place.

When I was a kid, the Boulevard seemed to go on forever. In my recurring dream the Boulevard took us to the end of the world. There was a grayish-pink sky where cars dropped off the edge of the world like a waterfall. What I remember of the dream's feeling is fear that my father had taken us too far as we struggled to turn around against the tide of traffic.

My father started working for SEPTA when he was 19. "I can't keep doing this, this bullshit," he would say to himself again and again over the years. He always intended to quit, find something better. He used to say, "A monkey could do my job." He took the Boulevard to work every day. He never quit.

SEPTA's slogan for decades has been "WE'RE GETTING THERE."

Plans for a Boulevard subway were revived in the 1960s, and Sears dug a tunnel for a station at Adams Avenue, where their catalog warehouse and a shopping center were located. But the city was denied federal funds and the project was abandoned.

Peggy West, my grandmother, remembers when the subway tunnel was being dug. She lived in Tacony, a neighborhood close by, along the river. Peggy loved public transportation. She was a country girl who fell in love with the city after falling in love with Chauncey West in the Navy.

Peggy was planning to go to Paris before Chauncey proposed to her. She was surprised—had figured she was already too old to get married—because she was 20. A far cry from Nebraska, Philadelphia seemed as good a future as any. "If I had gone to Paris," she told me, "you wouldn't be here."

In Chauncey's family, the dinner talk was a mix of worry, excitement and relief, propelled by continuous job insecurity—"did we get this contract, did we get that contract—they were neat but not happy stories," said Peggy.

The thing to do, Chauncey believed, having dropped out of high school and left the Navy, was to fall in love and move your family from North Philadelphia to Northeast Philadelphia—which is what hordes of white people were doing in the 1950s as more black people moved to the city.

Chauncey landed a union job with the Quaker Rubber company, which manufactured all kinds of hoses and things like escalator handrails for companies like Otis. And he got a house in Tacony, just north of the factory. He and Peggy raised their four daughters there. The eldest was Dorothy, my mother.

People in Tacony and Wissinoming were soon called "river rats" by people in Mayfair and neighborhoods developing farther north along the Boulevard. These white people, including the Italian and German immigrants of my father's family, took pride in having more income and a slightly larger patch of grass in front of their slightly larger house that was closer to a slightly nicer school and slightly more homogenous shopping center in a slightly more homogenous neighborhood that was slightly more distant from North Philly, where black people lived. They were more American, they thought, meaning better than everyone who lived south of them, while at the same time they worried that their own neighborhood was "changing" and would talk to each other quietly about moving to the next neighborhood north—"for the kids."

And so these white people were constantly abandoning what they said they believed in, which was their own superiority for having achieved middle-class status in their white skin in the country that had won World War II and created freedom for all—the freedom to fall in love and get a house with some grass in front of it and have kids you'll support by working a job that helps make the whole system go, a system that tells you and your kids in school that hard work will make you a good person, that you will get there.

I'm no river rat, Chauncey thought. But H.K. Porter, the giant train-maker, bought the rubber company and laid everyone off. And then Chauncey couldn't find a job, and he drank and drank and screamed at his daughters. Peggy went to work downtown as a secretary, typing a hundred words a minute. When she came home from work, Chauncey screamed at her, too. Dorothy took care of her younger sisters. Peggy and Chauncey divorced and a few years later, Chauncey died of aplastic anemia from exposure to chemicals in the factory.

Most people are horrified when they first encounter Roosevelt Boulevard, the spine of Northeast Philadelphia. It's a total free-for-all, a violent expression of 20th century masculine self-abandonment. Named after Theodore, it consists of twelve lanes, six up, six down, divided by two grass medians, some lined with trees, which open periodically for you to cross over at any speed you like—you can yield, sure, but it's not required. Your best bet, if the Boulevard is new to you, is to stay in a center lane so you can remain aware of drivers going 90 and 30 miles an hour. If you need to make a left turn, godspeed.

If you want to feel like the frog in Frogger, try crossing the Boulevard on foot. As a kid, I enjoyed the challenge. It's how I got to Tower Records. It's safer to jaywalk, using the medians to wait for cars to pass in either direction, rather than crossing at an intersection, where a car's quick left turn could end your life. It has in fact ended many lives.

The second- and third-most dangerous intersections in the United States are on the Boulevard. I grew up around the corner from the latter, Grant Ave and the Boulevard. Sometimes I heard accidents, and sometimes I heard stories of poor old ladies flying through the air. Up and down the Boulevard, year-round, the medians are decorated with flowers and crosses.

To reduce the number of accidents, the Philadelphia Parking Authority started a "Red Light Camera Program" that issues $100-tickets for blowing a red light. The program has resulted in huge profits for a private camera company in Arizona. It has not made the city safer.

The American solution to a public problem, created by private industry, is usually to find a new way to steal from the public. Robbing your neighbor, in other words, is an American tradition, and it thrives in Northeast Philly, where people live as if their neighbors do not really exist. Believing in the American dream is a way to deny your own existence.

Northeast residents actually saw themselves as so American that in the 1980s a state senator, Frank Salvatore, led a movement to secede the Northeast from Philadelphia. The Northeast was being robbed by the city, he believed. Our taxes are too high, he argued, for the paltry services we receive—not enough police, not enough trash collection, not enough street cleaning, not enough public transit. He proposed a bill that would make the Northeast, which was half-Republican, its own township: "Liberty Township." The dull, racist landscape would become all its own. The secessionist movement died, however, because it was unclear how Liberty Township would afford itself. The Northeast remains dependent on the rest of the city.

Not long before I moved out of the Northeast, I met the poet Gil Ott, who asked me about my life, what I wanted to do. He told me a story about getting lost once in the Northeast. "How does one get out of Northeast Philadelphia?" he asked. I said, "Do you mean if you're in a car or bus, or do you mean like culturally?" "Both," he said.

July 6, 2015

Dear Ryan,

I want you to have this badge. It was your Grandfather Chauncey's badge that he wore to work everyday that he worked, for 30 years. He was such a strong supporter of the United Rubber Workers of America and felt his shop union protected his job and benefits. He was shop steward for several years and when he was scalded in the manufacturing process one time, the union supplemented his pay for the six weeks he was on crutches. Of course, he never received his pension because the plant was sold and the new owner (H.K. Porter) denied the pension plan. I had heard that the union took the case to court, but by that time I was out of the picture and never heard the outcome. I suppose I could look it up on line if I had any idea where to look. Anyway, I have heard that you're not big on collecting things, but thought just maybe you would want to throw this in a drawer where it will occasionally remind you that you had a grandfather who was a guy who was big on unions, and who would be so very proud to see you doing the union work you are doing today. I often wonder if he would have any useful advice to offer you.

Love,

Grammy

Roxborough spur

There was a plan for a Roxborough spur that would parallel the Schuylkill River. It would run northwest from city hall under the Ben Franklin Parkway to the art museum, then up 29th Street, elevated, through North Philly, then along Henry Avenue out to Roxborough. The line would mirror the el—which exists—on the east side of the city, the extension of the Market-Frankford line that parallels the Delaware River, like an arm of the city.

To imagine a city truly of the people, I have to sense freedom in what's phantom. I imagine the Roxborough spur, for example, would have given the art museum two public arms. Would this have made the art museum more of a public space? And what would that mean?

Would it mean a place where people talk and make things together? Would it mean more nights like the Zoe Strauss opening, when there was a dance party, when the museum *was* Philly? Would it mean the museum would be free ("pay-what-you-want") more than one day a month? Would it mean everyone might have the means and time and interest to go there? Would it mean a completely different kind of museum from the ones we know?

At the end of Rocky V, after Rocky has taught his son how to fight, he says, "I've been running up these steps for twenty years and I never knew there were valuable pictures in this building."

Outside the museum, you can get your picture taken with a Rocky impersonator. Sometimes I see the impersonator out of character, as himself, walking around South Philly. I sat across from him on the subway once and two kids, maybe 15 years old, asked him for directions and they struck up small talk. "Where you headed?" they asked. "Work," he said. "What do you do?" "Oh, I'm a movie actor," he said. The kids just nodded. They didn't recognize him. He got off at city hall and then, presumably, made the 20-minute walk up the parkway to the art museum.

In New York City there's a man named Darius McCollum who's been impersonating transit employees for no money for over 30 years. He's been in and out of prison his entire adult life for criminal impersonation, without harming anyone. Obsessed with trains since he was a little kid, he knows how to operate and repair subways and buses and perform just about any MTA job. He has memorized the NYC subway map and schedules. He's even attended regular union meetings, sharing ideas for dealing with management and improving working conditions.

McCollum's obsession is blamed on Asperger syndrome, but the illnesses of our society have made his life impossible. He got picked on in school, and when he was 11 a classmate stabbed him in the back with scissors. He found refuge in the subway, befriending MTA employees who taught him how to operate the trains and used him happily as a source of free labor. McCollum, a black man, feels more at home in the subway than anywhere and knows more about the MTA than anyone. But the MTA refuses to offer him any type of job. They even refuse to let him volunteer at the MTA transit museum.

Last year McCollum was arrested for stealing a Greyhound bus and driving passengers, on time, to their scheduled destination. He is now facing up to 15 years, having already spent more than half of his adult life in prison. No matter how often McCollum is denied his identity as a public transit worker, he insists on it. He insists on his own belonging, unauthorized. He does not deny the facts, but he refuses the system's refusal of himself. He returns to the subway again and again as if to say "I am a part of you." And he is. He is actually *not* impersonating anyone.

The administrators of the city create a phantom and expect you to live in it. They expect you to become the phantom.

In high school, I loved escaping high school. Who didn't? Who doesn't? I loved riding the el downtown from Frankford, the motion pictures out the window, the old parks, factories and rooftops, the graffiti and feeling of racing through the city you were part of, unfolding with it—this was the feeling of leaving behind the prison of school, which was someone else's fantasy. The sudden swerve along I-95 and the slide underground at the Ben Franklin Bridge. I'd get off at 2nd Street and head down to South Street with my friends, looking for bootleg tapes of Nirvana and Pearl Jam shows. A store called CDs To Go let us listen on headphones to check the quality before we coughed up ten bucks for a recording on a blank tape. Then we'd make copies for each other, bring them back to school.

But that feeling on the el, which was a satisfaction of the need for movement, was a feeling of becoming something else, and that need to become something else is the need for public space, the need for *a public*, period. And I want to say that this need, which is also the need for collective power, unauthorized, is the only thing that can save us.

At the end of the phantom line, in Roxborough, retired cops get off I-76, stop at the supermarket for trash bags, drive home and park their private cars and walk their little dogs. They pick up their dogs' shit, cursing under their breath. They stay in school, as they always have, and they will die in school. Let them.

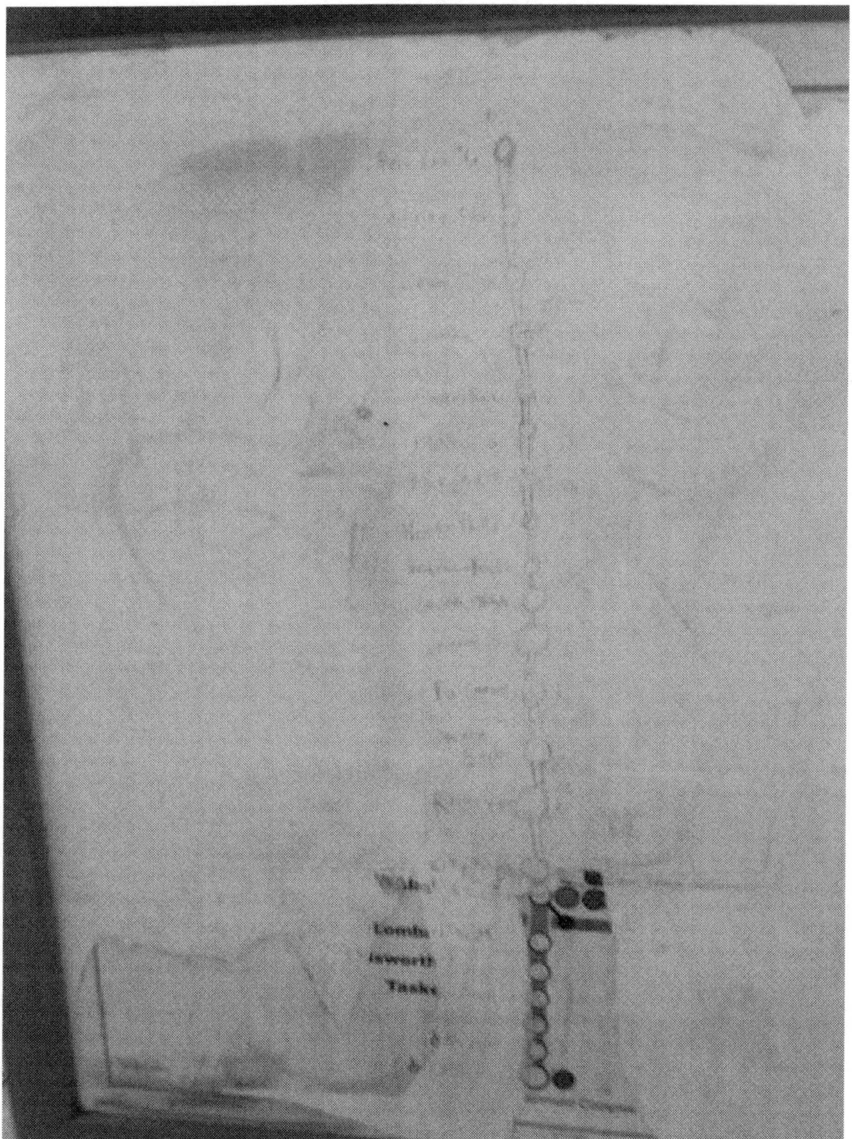

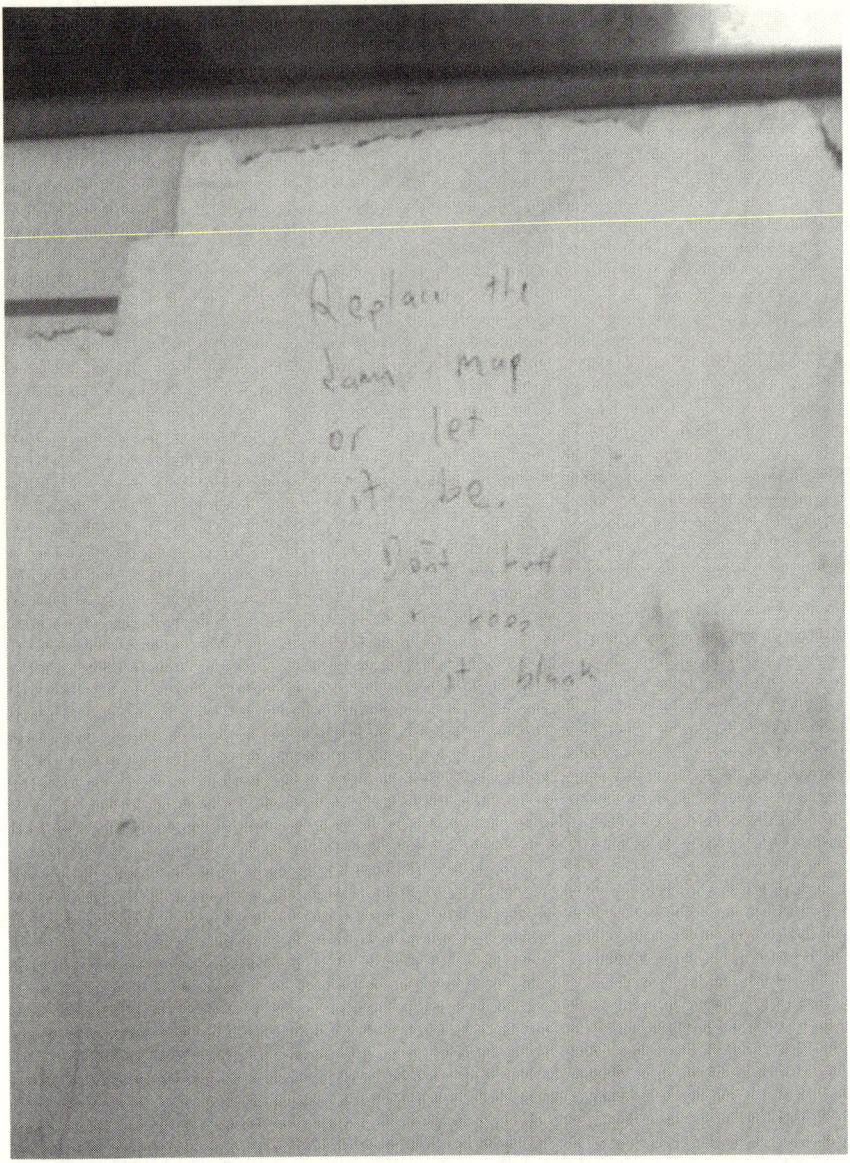
Replace the
damn map
or let
it be.
Don't
+ keep
it blank

III strikes

map

replace the damn map
or let it be
don't buff and keep it
blank
don't say love and be
there in spirit
don't ask how
my spirit is
if you got here
thru a suburb
officer
you were conceived
in this same lot
the king of jeans pulled
down his jeans and
it was your mouth
on the condo
replace the damn map
or let it be
don't buff and keep it
blank
i saved your life
and you gave me a six-pack
your life is worth a six-pack
to form   is to empty
the vent's lashes
are dogs running
i love you
for all time
the harmonica's
in my pocket
it plays   heart of gold
the dream   is at work
we get off   together
replace the damn map
or let it be
don't buff and keep it
blank

if fast food is public space
stay warm in wendy's
be a stranger
the stranger the weather the better
the small talk
a little history
a little ancient been-around
and biggie fry
you feel ancient
the ancient's been around
replace the damn map
or let it be
don't buff and keep it
blank
sit down
be a frosty
and sunny's the runniest dated feeling as
a weekend should be a long fuck sprawl
into other histories of meaning it
replace the damn map
or let it be
don't buff and keep it
blank
don't say love and be
there in spirit
don't dig up my street
get bored
and leave
turn the water back on
please
or the water will turn itself
the fuck back on
like i turn myself
the fuck back on
every day

dumper guard

to escape the great depression
people built roads
w/out a plan
my road is here
their road is there
you can guess
the state fish
slowly a letter
a day
the heart wants what
the car left
music
parked
in a train graveyard
in a forest
in north carolina
the shadow of an abandoned
staircase makes
public sense to
fuck under
hard work, scam
of life
back at you
four a.m.
dumper guard pours
money into milk cans
for septa
and his kids
jersey goes back
to jersey
and breaks off
into the ocean

secret service

you're telling me dolphins
aren't building cities
and killing everything
because they don't have hands
okay
the pope is in a jeep
w/ fins
waving to the dolphins
what's amore?
says a dolphin in a pope
t-shirt
smoking in the sea
i got this at a thrift store
in kentucky
on a road trip
it was raining
do you like it
do you like me
do you wanna strangle the sea
w/ these fins and rain and t-shirt
and everyone you've ever loved
and look
no hands
no hands

honk if you don't exist

a strike is people
the horse a door
you were saying
tempus fuck it
we made your car
it's an eraser
get in
sit, unknown, sit
honk
if you don't exist
you were saying
how to be anything
when everything's
exhaust
a parade of geese
has shut down
traffic in front
of the art museum
nobody honks
the traffic is thinking
about itself
its itness
my armpits
stink
my girlfriend
loves it
we're late
to a job
called food
the geese tease
the streets
the museum starts
jerking off
a cop shakes
his head
the steps collapse
into rain
rocky is now a girl
the flood hires us

to be water
our mouth
grabs the statue
of frank rizzo
by the ankles
he waves
goodbye
like a dead trophy
to his wife the cops
she was born cops
every day
a blue life
comes out of its
blue mom
a smurf w/ a gun
there's another one
mattering
like a sandwich
on a playground
marry me, he says, *marry me*
before drowning

christening

tired of songs
you show up in a true story
like a fist
the corner needs
& the corner needs
a new stop sign
so the city
which is two hired men
comes to change it
& in that bare minute
they retire the old
sign to their truck
a little dog comes along
& takes a quick piss
on the new one
right where it says
ALL WAY
and trots off

may day

what is may day
        bail paid in limes
behind wal-mart
the cat colony
jukes broken tracks
          apples
          hearts
          rolling in mud
small wolves
in chernobyl
woven awake
in marsh
   lush green
their crib an old
potato cellar
their mother looks out
of your house
        what is change
        what is change
without erasing yourself
        what will i eat
i will eat from your hands
where villages once stood
i will eat from the ground
your bison's last breath
i will trace the cold earth
i will trace the cold earth

dirty martini

it's like drinking the ocean
w/out choking
if life ended now
it's just time
ask me how
the whole city's doing
edgar allan poe is fine
in moyamensing prison
they love him
in the deli corner
of acme, muttering
provolone til the parking
lot is buried in snow
you can dig your car out
next week
here's a pack of tokens
and some scratch-offs
if you were born after
this day in 1912
you can bring the lovers
back together
one's walking into ray's
one's walking home right
now, probably a different
lorraine than the one
you know but all motion
is a crab, snockey's closed
and stays open
in my heart
which is late
to the tongue—take
my tongue and paint
their doors before
they're home, paint
their steps like
the bruises
you return to
as if employed
by orange peels

to the curb
you owe nothing
to the taste of
the weight
of desire, the city flattened
by rent as the rent dies
for our sins and the roads
bleed out

hold your horses

route 45 please
board at fire hydrant
under the shitty little birds
this must be you
coming from somewhere
how long's it been
since you named a thing
after a general
this pile of croutons
general croutons
we have passed the jetsons
and look, don't trip
the magic is not
olfactory
it's not my riff
you're smelling
it's the church of itch
got your tongue
between wires
there's a bite inside faith
like going to jury duty
we must repent
we must think again
like a pensive motherfucker
penser, i say
order in english
your big shit sandwich
for the neon coplover
in search of guitar
the shape of sound
blows horse shoes
in our direction
don't mind the cobble stone
don't mind the smoky job rot
pave over the track
all you want
the prison won't come back
you gotta drive around it
you gotta drive around it

to see the heart balloon
float across the rooftops
and disappear toward
the delaware

kazoo

cops in the apple store
working for "the city"
like you have to stay here
and be the place
no poem
so all mayors
must hang
as real ornaments
done to you
from trees parks
chalked up
all bodies make
a case for bracing
yourself, the city's lights
settle in your girl's
face who are fugitives
to grow us past mere
poetics
i am an ancestor too
who meant by "permanence"
(like a car)
food, shelter and sex
while performing abandonment
which is a door
in a cloud—open it
for the noose
made of bill gates
and watch bill move his mouth
over the toilet
40 public schools
into
one
your
assignment: write
an essay in which you crawl
toward subjectivity
as flat tires
gallop thru the wheezing
infrastructure

Spring Course Assignments

On Thu, Oct 1, 2015 at 7:52 PM, RYAN M. ECKES <eckes@temple.edu> wrote:

Hi Larry,

I just learned from Rachael Groner's email to FYWP about Spring course assignments that you're assigning courses in creative writing and literature for next semester. Is there a new availability form to fill out? I'd like to teach a course in the Spring.

Thanks,
Ryan

*

On Fri, Oct 2, 2015 at 7:08 AM, LAWRENCE VENUTI <lvenuti@temple.edu> wrote:

Dear Ryan,

All spring courses have been staffed. If you send me your c.v., I'll keep it on file in case anything becomes available.

Yours,
Larry

*

On Fri, Oct 2, 2015 at 1:15 PM, RYAN M. ECKES <eckes@temple.edu> wrote:

Larry,

I've been teaching here for 10 years. Every semester I've taught here the English Department has sent course request forms to adjunct professors to fill out for the following semester. Can you tell me why I wasn't invited to teach a course next semester?

Thanks,
Ryan

*

On Fri, Oct 2, 2015 at 1:23 PM, LAWRENCE VENUTI <lvenuti@temple.edu> wrote:

I'm sorry you feel singled out, Ryan. There were fewer courses to staff. If you send me a c.v., again, I'll keep it on file.

*

On Fri, Oct 2, 2015 at 9:32 PM, RYAN M. ECKES <eckes@temple.edu> wrote:

Larry,

My C.V., credentials, syllabi and evaluations should be on file. I've taught here for the last ten years.

Will you explain to me why you did not send out course request forms to English adjunct faculty for next semester? I am asking because this has been done for at least the last 20 semesters, and I was not notified of any change in procedure.

Also, it's odd that you used the term "singled out" in your email because being singled out hadn't occurred to me.

Ryan

*

On Fri, Oct 2, 2015 at 9:41 PM, LAWRENCE VENUTI <lvenuti@temple.edu> wrote:

You yourself implied that you were singled out, Ryan, because I had not contacted you personally. You wanted to know "why [you weren't] invited to teach a course next semester." That means that you were expecting a personal invitation.

61

I don't plan to send out course request forms to adjuncts. The volume of courses is too variable to satisfy all the requests that would come in.

The department keeps no file of c.v.s for adjuncts. I would like to maintain one. If you would like to send me yours, I'll include it.

*

On Tue, Oct 6, 2015 at 1:17 PM, RYAN M. ECKES <eckes@temple.edu> wrote:

Larry,

On what basis have you chosen to not offer me a course for the Spring?

Ryan

*

On Tue, Oct 6, 2015 at 1:20 PM, LAWRENCE VENUTI <lvenuti@temple.edu> wrote:

Dear Ryan,

Your messages to me have been filled with complaints. If you feel that you have grounds for complaint, please take up the matter with the department chair, Philip Yannella.

Yours,
Larry

Dear Adjunct Faculty:

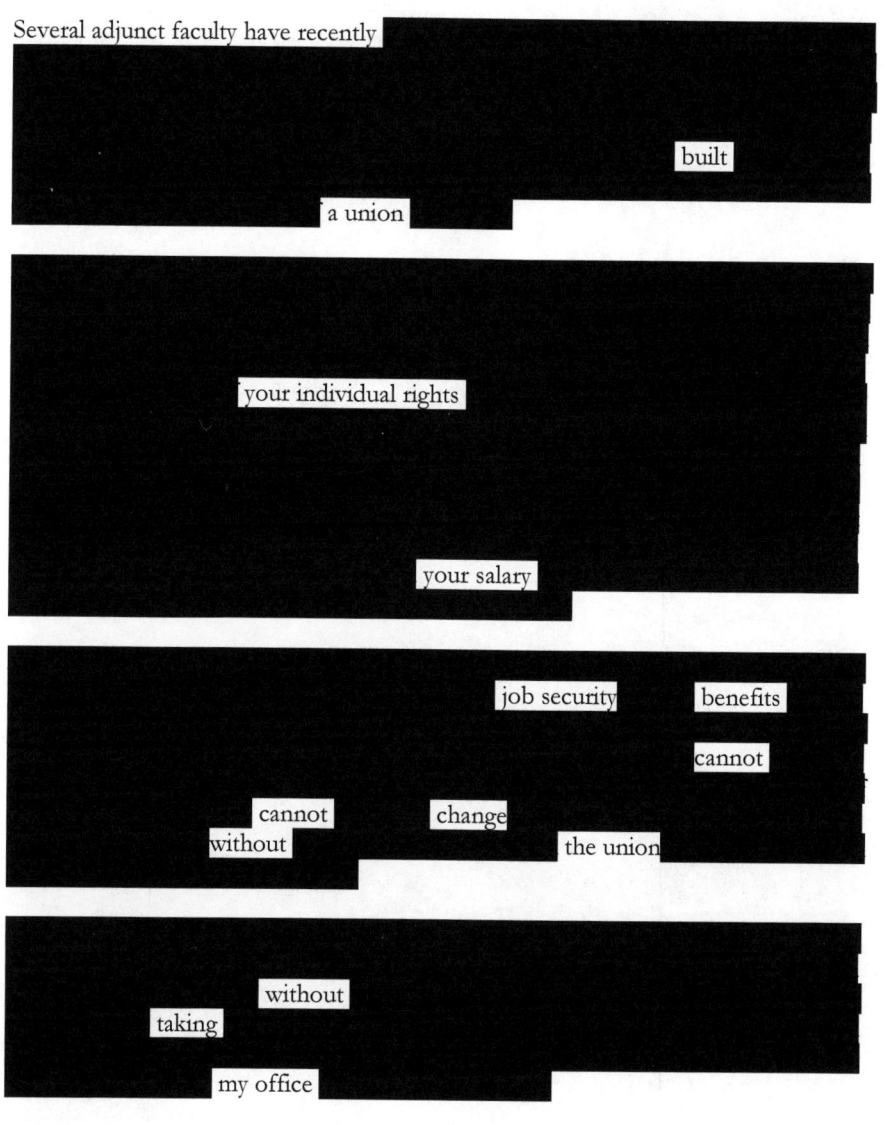

Several adjunct faculty have recently built a union

your individual rights

your salary

job security benefits cannot

cannot change
without   the union

without
taking
my office

Sincerely,

Provost and Senior Vice President for Academic Affairs
Temple University

bad form

99.9 percent of people eat their own god
but there's no word for it
because you keep checking your phone
how long have you worked
in this blue
who makes the decisions
in your blue
how much does the blue pay
why does your coke taste like
blood
what disrupts the illusion
if not the word "illusion"
which lulls us to sleep
it's all a bag of flowers
i grab a flower and brush the present
off my teeth
hillary clinton wants to be president
today
what are *you* going to do
you can't recall a knockoff
it's just a knockoff
in the united states of knockoff
you lost me at "i was born in . . ."
the block was blocked off
the cop said "i knew your dad back when"
and quoted us most of the collected everyone
"slavery is necessary," he said, "that's why
i'm voting for hillary"
then wiped his ass w/ a cat
and threw it at us
that's the god of life
just like you
on may day working
for the national poem
called "isolated consciousness looks at a tree"
at 6pm i went to lucky 13
drank nine blue coats
put a five on the bar
and walked out
bad form

bad form
gina had my back
paid the tab
said read "a broken world"
by joseph lease
an elegy for a friend
the opposite of a scab
in trust of death
a blackout is a small strike
don't make me make
meaning
don't make me walk out
the blue
of all time
after eating love
i will eat love again
my skin will be water
as yours
faith in rain
as rain and rain
as more than
love
don't make me
make words
for a solidarity
that works
so we all show up
as the tree yawning
down the isolated consciousness
of ernest hemingway
his knockoff armies
who will fight
for the wounded hero
in a pool of everyone else's blood
waving a flag of dicks
until the box office explodes
and all is profile pic
"what's on your mind?"
not you
and not you
and not you
and nothing
a bag of flowers

a block of us
talking to a hole
in the sky
the sky is scratched
nothing's crossed out
the cd plays
disparate youth
it skips
it's still good w/ the skips

memo for labor

you cannot separate the job from the house from the rent from the earth from the food from the healthcare from the water from the transit from the war from the schools from the prisons from the war from the water from the house from the healthcare from the war from the transit from the schools from the food from the job from the prisons from the rent from the earth

elevator no love

dear internet
world of non-action
goodbye
we're free
the temple's in the toilet
my keys are on the table
nobody's rich
and patter
in the dark
empty seats
thank god
we're a flea in a ferris wheel
we put a cap on the pomp
like a boss
made of water
here you cannot *teach*
for america
you will not cut out
your eyes
you will not cut off
your ears
and hang your balls
from the wire
for a name you can't feed
enough
there is no name
there is no *israel*
god is a football
roofed in the gutter
forever
a boy screams after it
until he is the scream
my gums bleed
in the morning
for new work
to circle the drain
"you" as no as loved
to the bottom
throws rocks at dead goalies

each rock a no
as the sky bruised into
question
no as the moon
if you wanna live
stop saying "sky"
and pick up a rock
and look at it

aida

i feel like i've died
feel like i've died
& gone to regular life
ray sings
on the tape deck
of aida's car
which is my car
aida was my grandmother
the tape plays over & over
it's a 97 toyota camry
aida bought for driving
to acme & dollar tree
once a week to use coupons
she clipped from the papers
watching tv w/ her cat
squirrels at her window
looking in
the reader wanting more
but finished crosswords
cigarettes, tissues & phlegm
acme & dollar tree
ray sings in aida's car
it's still aida's car
she was hard to get close to
the faint trace of her smoke
is now ray's sober voice
it warms me up
the tape is called *guts*
the band is called window kits
the song is called "whut yrmadeof"
ray isn't sure
he wonders aloud
he sings *these days i don't just let*
any old wind blow in
goddamn it, edie, i sing
in philip's voice
to ray's music
philip was my grandfather
he called his wife edie

the tape plays over & over
i drive thru new jersey
on house visits
i get one adjunct to sign
an authorization card
UNION YES
we want better pay
we want healthcare
we want a voice
in regular life
hey, how are you
it's regular life
good pay, job security
& healthcare
no reason to move
ever again
i will live in this house
for 60 years
& clip coupons
for my cat
it's a 97 toyota camry
beige or something
faint trace of window
kits thru new jersey
my guardian angel
in the ashtray
cigarette burns
on the door
heaven is a place
where nothing ever happens
imagine if we threw out
the scumbags who run
our schools
imagine if WE ran the schools
yeah
what then
right
yeah
sounds good
power in numbers
see you later
and i'm still writing songs about ghosts
ray sings

ray's still sad
i give a eulogy for aida again
because no one else will
they're too afraid
their histories too fraught
too painful but for me
she was distant enough
i can make everyone
happy w/ a mild honesty
about her 97 years
of life
so listen
she helped me one time
w/ a paper on the great
depression in middle school
there was a detail
about rumble-seating
on broad street
a detail she repeated over & over
until crystallized
aida laughing down broad street
thru hard times
that's who she was, people
this fierce wild-at-heart woman
who loved to travel & explore
& play by her own rules
tough as anything
that's right
no words
on the way
she treated her children
nothing on why
they can't speak
at her funeral
in regular life
goddamn it, edie
stop telling us how to live
the war is over
you won
the poem is in my back
like a knot
the pain is returning
as a ripple

the job's no longer
fulfilling
what is regular life
why do you believe in it
another week
a slab of meat
slapped on top
some cheese
sixty hours of regular life
that's a freedom sandwich
a sandwich for freedom
imagine the pleasure of biting
into permanent holiday
which is why i've worked
so hard
& my father
& my grandfather
& my mother
& my grandmother
& everyone's grandmother
saving up what they can
for the boxes
they'll never own
which hide the ripples
one life to another
a union
a sea
a city
of body as ripple
in another
& *of* another
& no eulogy
no coupon
for your grave
but the whole story as city openly
made together
over & over
i think of anna
how are you
right now
other side of the river
doing the same thing
cars pass

people don't answer
i pretend you're next to me
we talk about ripples
all kinds
we theorize it
til you laugh & say no
w/ your lips
which i trace w/ my finger
for weeks
it's my dream
it's watery
i stare at the ocean
on my wall
it's night
& seagulls squawk by
in the sky outside
for what
just passing thru
it's winter
a line of glue
streak of sense
spine in dream
on my way
to this job of loving
outside a box
i wanna say something
like *we've been cultured out of the primordial*
now sign this card, okay
but that won't work
ask saul alinksy
ask anybody
this union
what is it
what is it
really
is it desire
clumsy
sloppy
desire
what i want
from you
is what i want
for you

my heart
which is nothing
but all my
wanting
for all that radiates
care &
pleasure &
hunger for knowing unfolding &
pulsing &
coming
in spite of the shoulder-
stooping fear that radiates
from shards of dead intimacy
& violence along my spine
the dotted lines of the road
no after no after no
echo from those dim hallways
of those dull buildings
we spent all those years in
trying to speak
all the muted tv's
of the world
still
anything can happen, you said
in the bar
in the glow
to my face
no one's going anywhere
it's true
even parallel parking can
be the sexiest
thing
push your ass
against the bumper
hop the curb
grab my head
cut the wheel
say what you want
down my tight
street
straddled & pulsing
i just slide right in
so serious, you say,

so serious
as regular life begins
to disappear
we wake up
our union keeps
winning
harder & harder
we joke
it's the slogan
we like it
we want it
on a t-shirt
we want it
turned inside-out
tossed to the floor
over & over
a ball rolls
down the street
so kick it
to be alive
in other ways
how my body
aches
for what we can't yet be
how your name
when i see it
burns
how your smell
how your ache
how your lips
how your hurt
when you hurt
      is mine
how your hurt
when i hurt
      is this
how the hurt
when it hurts
      is ours

baptism

a factory makes facts
you show up
then you're gone
red clouds eat
the snow
inside me
like a footprint
june is purple
drums are rooms
for infinite need
the lungs walk out
in four decades
52% of wildlife gone
where to park
that stone whale
in a moon of notes
i get by
like the news
under hums
in the shape of a squirrel
a man may form
and fall from a tree
an apple
flashing the sky
between our huts
fish teeth
are a secret
baptized
w/out a bus
to splash into
your eye in the skull
of a penguin
clocks out the city
like a dad who sighs
up the stairs
gray whir of traffic
underlining the past

it's all for us
minus the job clown
on your shoulder

Same Time

In cold war school, fourth grade, we had "current events." We performed newscasts in class, took turns reporting what we'd found at home from the newspaper. And then, I guess, we talked about it. Today we do this as adults on facebook and twitter.

-

There was a massive strike in India last Friday. The fact squeaked through all the plutocratic noise, a blip I've clung to as infinite. Would you tell me about it?

-

Indiana Jones, tumbleweed, rolls down the street, totally whole. Don't look back, Mr. Jones. Take all the Dr. Phils with you, turn down a side street and I will meet you there with open trash bag.

-

"The universe will never happen," says Heriberto Yépez. I love the closure as how many millions open other books the same time I close mine.

-

When I hear "universe" I think "union." I scrape the bottom of a jar with my spoon, a dry tongue.

-

It's not what I'm missing that hurts, but this endless need to become something else against mass expression of collective powerlessness.

-

Enough, clearly, is not enough.

-

the pears are the pears
the table is the table
the house is the house
the windows are the windows

the car is the car
the roads are the roads
the streets are the streets
the white line is the white line

the curves are the curves
the thigh is the thigh
the knee is the knee
the arms are the arms

the eyes are the eyes
the mouth is the mouth

-

Ted Greenwald said that. It got me here, the poem, dropped me off, hey thanks for the ride.

-

The mouth is a way out
The moon is a fat dime
Exact change only

-

I was there in the painting with the gulls on the rock. We wrote our names on the rock to be there with each other.

-

"Common" means moving + changing together.

-

"I miss your angry heart," you text from across the country, working.

"I miss your angry heart," I text back, working.

-

"We cobbled it together," I said about another relationship. When I talk about my working life, I say "I've cobbled it together."

-

Our lives paved by gigs, the news evaporates quickly. The ground is shaky. Shaky quickly, we heart our friends' transmissions. Do these tiny solidarities add up?

-

There's no such thing as a "gig" economy. It's a scab economy, long been, sustained by capitalist government.

-

I like it when all my friends post pictures of the sunset at the same time.

-

Will we find a way to throw our cobbles at the right people at the same time?

-

During the Q&A of a recent poetry reading, older poets started talking about dodge ball as if it were a game that younger poets had never played, as if the game were extinct.

-

"Common" means moving + changing together.

-

When I was a kid we played a game in the schoolyard called "suey"—short for suicide, I learned later—in which we pegged the shit out of each other with a tennis ball. The more you dropped the ball, the more you got pegged.

-

Gus, the Pennsylvania lottery groundhog, says "Keep on scratchin!"

-

If you see your own shadow, it means love as refusal. It means love as refusal so you can drag your sorry ass out of bed in the morning.

-

"Common" means moving + changing together.

-

We organized our shadows into love as refusal, and the day followed. We dodged the boss and laughed towards a plan.

-

Imagine being more than affect in a time of mic drops.

-

Is this thing on?

-

Let's sit down and watch our pay go up.

burnt turf

record is mint
12.99
it's yours, somebody
in nebraska loves you
"the flower's always
in the almond," evaporates
steamboat willie on my street
w/ xylophone teeth
there's infinite parking
put eyelashes on your car
and spit
i like that
ungentrified wink
unknotting my back
like an old lover
in that faded way
it's contagious
the echo
of shadow
coming off you
in sheets, hips
pulled against me
in waves
of houses
lie down w/ the ghost
wake up w/ the ghost
i was dead for a long time
but look, sunday, my clothes
on the radiator are dry
and my heart is public, ripe
for the cellar that goes on
and on so we can keep chasing
ourselves into the ground
in all directions twentieth
centuries, how these rotting
bridges can hold up train after
train of coal and death, steel
veins rusting out of concrete
each train a need to keep

pushing outward
you hear it at night
in the wind
three whistles
basic desire
the bouncing ball
keeping time
you can squeeze the benjamin franklin
house between two parking meters
and feed the art world for two seconds
and pretend the end of history
falling asleep convinced
that love is whatever can speak
for the emptiness and scribble it
down for permanence
and fall asleep again, trains
for some, cars for others
general motors for all
our grinding teeth and
wal-mart in the back
in the morning
no strike but
a loose dream
of a circulation
that equals solidarity
instead of these neighborhoods
bumbling w/ little yuppie kids
in halloween costumes
they are balloons
we must pop
open your books, children, to chapter
1: *letting go of status*
a motorcycle farts off the car alarms
and laughter becomes us, the street, vein of
endless transfer we celebrate
no state but the seed within
chapter 2: *sell the moon for a seven-minute
cartoon called "fuck the boss"*
which will grow roots
that tunnel out a vast
subway system so people
can get to pleasure
on time in every part

of town—this is my plan
for the city
it already happened
it's called "burnt turf"
record is mint
the cars pulled us
all apart finally
we stopped stumbling
out of work
and built new bridges
from the corpses
of meter maids
i mean millionaires
and walked them
and walked them again
a million here, a million there
burnt turf
record is mint
i woke up in the backseat
of a car
crossing grays ferry
it was my dead grandmother
don't worry, she said
tossed her cigarette out the window
it's the future, she said, broke means
together now
and drove on in silence
for a long time
i stared out the window
we were there
and love ceased to be an escape

bibliography

Bianco, Martha J. "Kennedy, 60 Minutes, and Roger Rabbit: Understanding Conspiracy-Theory Explanations of The Decline of Urban Mass Transit." *Center for Urban Studies Publications & Reports*. Portland State University. 1998.

Bruder, Michael. "Going Under: Inside a phantom SEPTA subway station." *Philly Voice*, 4 Nov. 2015, www.phillyvoice.com/inside-septas-phantom-subway-stops/

Freemark, Yonah. "Transit for a Future Philadelphia." *The Transport Politic*, 8 April 2009, www.thetransportpolitic.com/2009/04/08/transit-for-a-future-philadelphia/

Goddard, Stephen B. *Getting There: The Epic Struggle between Road and Rail in the American Century*. Basic Books, 1994.

Kwitny, Jonathan. "The Great Transportation Conspiracy: A juggernaut named desire." *Harper's Magazine*, Feb 1981.

Off the Rails. Directed by Adam Irving. The Film Collaborative, 2016.

Philadelphia (Pa.) Dept. of City Transit. *Annual Report*. 1914.

Pompilio, Natalie. "Secede? The idea is faint, but not yet dead." *The Philadelphia Inquirer*, Nov 17, 2004.

Tietz, Jeff. "The Boy Who Loved Transit: How the system failed an obsession." *Harper's Magazine*, May 2002.

"Urbex Photographer Discovers Eerie 'Train Graveyard' in North Carolina Forest." *PetaPixel*, 31 July 2014, petapixel.com/2014/07/31/urbex-photographer-discovers-eerie-train-graveyard-north-carolina-forest/

Who Framed Roger Rabbit. Directed by Robert Zemeckis. Touchstone Pictures, 1988.

Wolfinger, James. *Philadelphia Divided: Race and Politics in the City of Brotherly Love*. The University of North Carolina Press, 2007.

acknowledgments

The map at the beginning of the "spurs" section is from the Annual Report of the Department of City Transit for the City of Philadelphia for the year ending December 31, 1914.

The photographs at the end of the "spurs" section were taken at the Ellsworth-Federal Station of the Broad Street Subway in 2014.

In "Same Time," the poem by Ted Greenwald is "The Pears Are the Pears" from Greenwald's book *Common Sense* (L Publications, 1978).

Thank you to the editors of the following publications, in which parts of this book previously appeared:

Tripwire: a journal of poetics
Slow Poetry in America newsletter
Entropy
Sundog Lit
The Brooklyn Rail
Public Pool
Whirlwind Magazine
Supplement
Sugar Mule
Jámpster
Boneless Skinless
The William & Mary Review
The Trinity Review
Dusie blog
Argos Poetry Calendar

Thank you to Carlos Soto-Román, who translated some of these poems into Spanish for the chapbook *Patriotismo* (Libros del Pez Espiral, Santiago, Chile, 2016).

Thank you to The Pew Center for Arts & Heritage for a fellowship that gave me time to complete this book.

And thank you to my friends & to my family. You all keep me going.

Ryan Eckes is a poet from Philadelphia. He wrote *General Motors* from 2013-2016. His other books include *Valu-Plus* and *Old News* (Furniture Press 2014, 2011). He has worked as an adjunct professor at numerous colleges and in recent years as a labor organizer in education. He is the recipient of a 2016 Pew Fellowship in the Arts.

NOW AVAILABLE FROM

Split Lip Press

Fruit Mansion
by Sam Herschel Wein

Felt in the Jaw
by Kristen Arnett

Antlers in Space and Other Common Phenomena
essays by Melissa Wiley

I Once Met You But You Were Dead
by SJ Sindu

Plastic Vodka Bottle Sleepover
by Mila Jaroniec

For more info about the press and our titles, please visit:

WEBSITE: www.splitlippress.com
TWITTER: @splitlippress

AND DISCOVER MORE IN

Find great literature, music, fine art and film by visiting:

WEBSITE: www.splitlipmagazine.com
FACEBOOK: facebook.com/splitlipmagazine
TWITTER: @splitlipthemag